THE
SPORT
PARENT'S
MANUAL

WHAT YOUNG ATHLETES REALLY WANT THEIR PARENTS TO KNOW!

BY TOM DOYLE

www.truecoaching.net
206-919-4693

SAN JUAN PUBLISHING
P.O. Box 923
Woodinville, WA 98072
425-485-2813
sanjuanbooks@yahoo.com
www.sanjuanbooks.com

© 2006 by Tom Doyle

Publisher: Michael D. McCloskey
Design and production: Jennifer Shontz
Editor: Sherrill Carlson

ISBN 0-9707399-5-8
(ISBN-13: 978-0-9707399-5-7)

First Printing 2006
10 9 8 7 6 5 4 3 2 1
Printed in United States of America

TABLE OF CONTENTS

INTRODUCTION

Parents have a particularly difficult task. No one ever taught us how to be parents other than through example. There is no training period, only on-the-job training. There is no evaluation process as we go. To top it all off, our kids keep getting older, bigger, stronger, faster, and smarter, thus forcing us to continually readjust our parental policies and procedures. Usually after our children are raised, we wish we had done some things differently.

This booklet offers insights on how to work with your children, how to motivate them, how to understand and communicate with them just a little better. This parent guide is designed to offer insight into the many different perspectives in your lives and those of your children as well as offer some suggestions on parenting an athlete in the 21st Century. As is often the case with material like this, some of the ideas will be immediately applicable to your parenting; some will not be as useful in your particular situation. Take what works for you and enjoy the experience of raising athletic children just a little bit more.

HAPPY PARENTS

A common thought among coaches is the ideal place to coach would be an orphanage. They would be able to coach kids without having to interact with parents. It is difficult to keep everyone in an athletic program happy, especially parents who only want the best for their kids. Some coaches suggest there is only one strategy for keeping parents happy with their son or daughter's athletic experience:

How can a coach keep the parents of an athlete happy?
◆ Play their kid
◆ Play their kid all the time
◆ Play their kid all the time and WIN

Of course, we all know this is not possible. In fact, many athletic directors give out 3x5 cards to parents at their Annual Basketball Parent Nights and ask them to write down how many minutes they think their son or daughter ought to play per game. Keep in mind there are 8 minutes in a quarter, 32 minutes in a game, and 160 total minutes for five players on the floor. Then they add up the totals. Inevitably, the number is far greater than the available number of minutes.

What does that tell us?

It tells us parents sometimes have unrealistic expectations of their child's skills or of the purpose of a high school program. Parents too often think the lessons of high school athletics can only be taught on the floor, the course, the field, or in the pool during contests – that practice doesn't count for anything.

It tells coaches there is going to be conflict. In some cases the fear of this potential conflict either chases coaches out of the business or coerces them into keeping fewer players on a team with the hope the coach can keep this smaller number of kids happy.

It tells us kids' ideas have changed as well. It used to be that kids were happy and satisfied just being on a team. Some of you can remember seasons where teams' Most Valuable Players were players who never (or almost never) got on the floor in a contest. Their teammates voted them the MVP because they practiced every day as if it were their game. They made the rest of the team improve because they pushed them so hard day after day. The whole team benefited from their attitude. Today, kids often think there is no point participating if they are not playing. Who benefits more, the kids who participated and practiced every day or the ones who quit because they didn't want to sit on the bench?

What do we really want our kids to get out of their high school athletic experience? Are we looking for the college scholarship, the recognition, the attention? Or are we hoping they learn something about themselves and their relationships with others? Are they not learning how to compete? How to challenge themselves to be better, to improve? How to push themselves when they really don't feel like doing it today? How to give of themselves so someone else can benefit? The victory of the "WE" over the "I?"

We should all be thrilled our kids are participating in high school sports. Period! They are occupying time, learning, and staying out of other troubles. They are a part of something much bigger than themselves and potentially very positive. They are making friends, learning about themselves, learning to cooperate with peers, learning to deal with a "boss," both when that boss is positive and when the boss is negative. Lots of life-long lessons are taught every day at practice in all sports. Too often, we are looking at the "end" and miss the journey.

It is the journey that makes participation worthwhile. The journey can be a very difficult one; yet that makes it more honorable and worthwhile. The key word in the saying "play my kid" is "play." This is supposed to be an adventure filled with excitement. If you remember watching your young children play, they were very, very serious about the actions of the adventure. Your child probably came home dirty and sweaty, maybe even sore, but anxiously wanting to share stories of all the fun.

Play, being on a team, is hard work. One can either "play at working" or "work at playing." Which would you like your athlete to do? After teaching for 30 years, I saw way too many kids who "play at working," who don't understand it takes sweat and tears to be successful. When you "play at working," you can quit and move on to something that isn't so much work. I saw too many students who "played at working" on their studies and never did more than was asked and often did less, because it was too hard. I also saw many students and athletes who understood they had to work hard – that play wasn't always fun and games, that the fun came after the hard work, when the results were in. During my college football days, I don't ever remember games as fun. They were hard, painful experiences. The fun resulted from being prepared, from picking myself up when I got knocked down, from playing well, and from the relationships with others on the team. My daughter, a five-time state champion swimmer, understood this. She loved practicing and only tolerated competition. She loved pushing herself to be better and faster and stronger. She loved the friendships with coaches and other swimmers. Competition was a necessary evil to find out how much she had progressed and how much there was yet to do. Others only remember the relationships with others. Those years where the team gets along well and appreciates each other are wonderful. Those years filled with conflict among teammates, even in winning seasons, are painful. Some remember the fun is in the competition itself. The challenge of putting yourself out there and competing to the best of your ability provides enough satisfaction for them. All these experiences require a personal commitment to be successful and meaningful.

We should be honoring those who try, who strive to be better, to succeed, to win. We need to let go of the personal need and expectations that cause us to demand our kids be on the court or playing field during a contest and we need to understand why high school sports exist. Only then will parents be truly happy.

CHALLENGES IN ATHLETICS TODAY

Does it seem like high school sports are different than when you were playing, that there is more pressure now, that high school sports can be more fanatical than even a few years ago? Perusing the newspaper, we see articles about a cheer parent in Texas shooting a cheerleader after her own daughter did not make the squad; a parent who comes out of the stands and attacks a coach after a game; two parents who fight each other in the stands after comments about which of their kids should be the starting running back; the T-ball coach of a team of 8-year olds who paid one of his players $25 to beat up a teammate with mental challenges so he wouldn't be able to be in the game for the league required three innings. Has competition gone way too far? What problems are we experiencing today?

Surveying differences in athletics over the last couple decades, we find there are fewer athletes turning out for high school sports than one would expect. More athletes are quitting at an earlier age as a result of the pressure and burnout of little league, traveling, and select programs. Sports are just no fun anymore for these kids. A 2005 Maine study suggests 72% of all kids playing little league sports quit before they get to high school. Is this a healthy situation?

There are fewer and fewer qualified officials as the numbers of men and women choosing to work in this capacity drops. As competitive levels and pressures increase, the demands on officials grow exponentially as well. Officials are harassed, abused, in some cases attacked, and, in almost all cases, criticized for every call they make. In some areas in the country, there are no longer enough officials to work all the games schools want to play. Athletic directors must call the official's assignor before scheduling a contest to make sure of the availability of someone to work the contest. In the not-too-distant past, most refs used to be school personnel – now very few are. So a man or woman must leave their "regular" job early to officiate an afternoon contest and then, to top it all off, they must subject themselves to the abuse they will receive for their paltry fee earned working the game. Why would anyone want to do this?

Parents used to accept the fact that playing on a team was a privilege, not a right; that the coach was the decision maker; and that their place was in the stands. Today, parents believe it is critical for their kids' futures that they not only are on a team, but that they play and be a star. The coach is no longer always right. In fact, there are probably more dinner table conversations about the coach's ability and strategic decisions than ever before. Parents no longer sit quietly in the stands; now they feel they have a right to provide input on every decision the coach makes from offensive strategy to starting lineups. A parent 20 years ago would say, "the coach is always right." Today, this saying might change to, "I have coached, I know the game, and I think the coach is going about this in the wrong way." Parents feel they have a right and responsibility today to "go to the top" and speak with administrators when their child is unhappy with an athletic experience. How does this change in attitude affect our sons' and daughters' perspective of their coaches?

It used to be there was a sense among parents that youth was a time for growing up and that the kids needed to experience some failure in order to learn how to deal with it. Today, parents are concerned about their kids getting into the right school or the right profession or the right group. Any blemishes on their record or any failures might prevent the athlete from attaining this goal. So parents now fight to protect their children from the consequences of failure. They act out of a misguided sense of love to protect them from this most needed measure of learning. It is a cliché, but we know we learn the most from our mistakes. In order to learn from mistakes, we have to make some, and then deal with the results. We too often preach this cliché, but then don't allow it to be practiced. What message do we give our kids when we fix all their problems and, in essence, tell them they are not capable of handling the problems themselves? That is not what our intent is, but, in fact, it is the message we send when we step in as their protectors. Are we letting our kids grow up?

More coaches are quitting each year. The newspaper will generally report a coach quit to spend more time with the family. This is "code" for "the parents are out of control and I can't deal with it anymore." Coaches, like officials, used to be teachers. Today, more and more coaches come not from the educational arena, but from business. Where teachers often were specifically trained in dealing with young people, those coming out of business have to learn it in other ways. Out-of-building coaches experience their athletes at practice, but don't often have the opportunity to see how they interact with others during the day or to talk with their teachers and counselors about how they are doing in school. It gets tougher every day for an athletic director to fill a coaching position. How many people with "real jobs" (as opposed to teachers!) are available from 2pm – 10pm on a daily basis, especially when one considers the low salaries offered for these positions?

Sportsmanship may be at an all-time low. Can it go lower or will we turn the corner and get back in control? Violence at contests is more prevalent: Athletes fighting, spectators attacking officials, student fights in the parking lot after a contest. Where does it all stop?

Many of these changes have occurred in the last 5-10 years. If the trend keeps up, where will we be in another 5 years? Can we afford to wait and see or must we act now to ensure these trends don't continue? As a parent, what is your responsibility? Is it someone else's job or do you share in it as a role model for your sons, daughters, and their teammates? Hopefully, you can answer this rhetorical question with a resounding commitment to improving the situation.

PERCEPTIONS = REALITY?

There isn't time and space here for an entire explanation of the difference between perception and reality. Suffice it to say the way we perceive things to be is not always accurate. We may think we understand clearly what is happening, but we may not see the whole picture. The danger in any relationship comes from our belief that our perception is reality, that it is unfailingly accurate. We get into conflicts with others (a spouse, a child, a coach, a teacher, a business associate) precisely because we look at the same stimulus and see it from different perspectives. Perhaps one of the best examples of this is an exercise from a Lou Tice (founder of the Pacific Institute) presentation in the early 1970's. Take a look at the following sentence and count the number of "F"s you see:

FINISHED FILES ARE THE
RESULT OF YEARS OF SCIENTIFIC
STUDY COMBINED WITH THE
EXPERIENCE OF MANY YEARS

What number did you come up with in your count? Be honest! Did you see three? Four? Five? Six? If shown to a group of people, most will say three, a few will see four, a few five, and a smaller number will see six. In fact, there are six. The "F" in the word "OF" is commonly left out of the count. First of all, it sounds like a "v", not an "f", and secondly, we are taught to read right through the little words, the little things, when we learn to read. So it is easy to understand why most people think there are three "f"s. How is it we all see the same sentence, words, and letters, yet we answer the question differently? What effect does it have on communication when we sometimes miss the "little things" (like the "f"s in "of")? Could it be our perception may not always be correct and others may see things differently (and maybe more correctly)? Horrors!

Remember the sentences with the "F"s any time you find yourself making judgments about others or about situations involving your athlete and the coach. Take a second look. You may be correct, but you may also have made one of those judgments based on erroneous perceptions.

MISSION STATEMENT
OF YOUR SCHOOL

Take a look at your school's Mission Statement. Why do high school sports exist? Most mission statements will emphasize the following in some form or another:

♦ To work with others—The Victory of the WE over the I.
♦ To be successful—"We do not always win, but we succeed when we continually STRIVE to WIN. Winning is not everything, but making the effort to win is!" —Vince Lombardi
♦ To develop sportsmanship.
♦ To improve—skill development strengthens self-image.
♦ To enjoy athletics.
♦ To develop desirable personal health habits.

What is interesting is what is not there. It would be very difficult to find a high school program indicating in its Mission Statement that it is a goal of the athletic experience to: 1) obtain scholarships for athletes; 2) gain personal publicity and recognition for an individual athlete; or 3) win league, district, regional, or state championships. These may be by-products of the experience, but they are not the reason athletics exist in schools. Outside organizations, like select and traveling teams, may suggest they can accomplish these goals – but schools do not. Parents need to understand this and accept high school athletics for what it is – a laboratory where student-athletes learn many valuable life lessons whether they start or come off the bench, whether their team wins or loses.

WHY DO STUDENTS PARTICIPATE IN SPORTS?

Why do you think your son or daughter plays a high school sport? Have you ever actually had this type of conversation with your athlete? It might be a worthwhile experience for both of you! According to a Michigan State University study conducted in the 1989, kids play for the following reasons:

WHY DO BOYS PLAY?
1. To have fun
2. To do something I am good at
3. To improve my skills
4. For the excitement of competition
5. To stay in shape
6. For the challenge of competition
7. To get exercise
8. To learn new skills
9. To be part of a team
10. To go to a higher level of competition

WHY DO GIRLS PLAY?
1. To have fun
2. To stay in shape
3. To get exercise
4. To improve my skill
5. To do something I am good at
6. To learn new skills
7. For the excitement of competition
8. To play as part of a team
9. To make new friends
10. For the challenge of competition

It is worth noting what is #1 for both sexes. Now one has to define and, maybe, debate what is meant by the word "fun," but clearly it is something different from competition, which comes further down the line for both boys and girls.

Parents ought to have conversation with their sons/daughters to find out exactly why they are playing a sport before they start. Are they playing because they want to or because they feel pressure from their parents to play? How motivated will they be if they are playing for their parent's reasons instead of their own?

During the season, the parents ought to remember it is the athlete's opportunity for an experience, not theirs. Allow them to enjoy this experience. Listen to their stories, their joys, and their complaints. But remember it is their experience, not yours.

After contests, parents should allow some time to pass before talking with their son or daughter about the contest. Kids need time to unwind, to move past the competition, to evaluate themselves and their performance, and to "come down" after the excitement of competition. Give them time.

SPORTSMANSHIP

Like it or not, you are a role model for your athlete. It is critical that you demonstrate good sportsmanship at all times, most importantly when you least feel like it. Webster's Dictionary defines sportsmanship as, "the ability to take a loss without complaint or a victory without gloating, and to treat opponents with fairness, generosity, and courtesy."

Why is it so critical? First of all, it is the right thing to do. High school sports are not synonymous with combat. Sporting events provide a chance for 14-18-year-old kids to demonstrate their skills and to test what they have learned. They are not life or death situations, they do not prove anything about whether the winner or loser is a better person. The right thing to do is to treat the opponents, the officials, the game, and yourself with respect. If we do this, we can all walk away from a high school contest with dignity, win or lose.

Being a good sport is also the right thing to do for safety's sake. When the game becomes more than a game, then egos are on the line and, sometimes people react poorly when their egos are damaged. Violence at contests is a result of one side showing no respect for another. The attendant lack of dignity then causes the other side to strike back, to try to "save face" by winning the "extracurricular" activities after the game. No one wins when this occurs. Sportsmanship is the best antidote.

What does good sportsmanship look like? Wake County Public Schools in North Carolina engage in a program they call "High Fives to Sportsmanship."

They suggest people who practice good sportsmanship do the following:

1. Show respect for the opponents at all times
2. Show respect for the officials.
3. Know, understand, and appreciate the rules of the contest.
4. Maintain self-control at all times.
5. Recognize and appreciate skill in performance regardless of affiliation.

Is this too much to ask of adults who are role models for their children? One final thought about spectators. Again referring to Webster's Dictionary for help, a spectator is defined as, "one who watches without taking an active part." Everyone has a role in a contest: The players play; the referees officiate; the coaches coach; and the parents "spectate." As Bruce Brown, a motivational speaker for the National Association of Intercollegiate Athletics (NAIA), says, "Parents want to coach; coaches want to officiate; officials want to watch. You can only do one. CHOOSE!" Choose what your athletes need most. They have a coach, they have officials — what they need most from you is a parent or guardian who will love them and appreciate them for who they are. Be a parent. Choose wisely.

RELATIONS WITH COACHES

Keep in mind there are natural conflicts between coaches and parents. Parents' primary concern is for their own son or daughter. A coach's primary concern is for the team. Coaches emphasize the "we" over the "I." Parents, while supportive of the team, are mainly concerned with the successes and failures of their own flesh and blood.

Parents have long-term goals for their children: to graduate from high school; to go to college; to get a decent job. Coaches' goals tend to be more short-term: the practice; the contest; the season. Coaches certainly are also concerned about the long-term development of those they coach, but their time frame is more limited than parents'.

Coaches might operate out of the "no pain, no gain" philosophy of life. They believe athletes who experience pain and frustration will actually be stronger as a result of it and learn a great deal more because of it. Parents, who have to sit at the same dinner table with a son or daughter who is in either physical or psychological pain, often try to protect their child from experiencing pain. After a long day at work, parents want a calm atmosphere at home. The pain of conflict with a team or coach isn't always appreciated around the house.

Conflict exists. We must deal with it. How much better it would be to find positive ways for dealing with it rather than heightening the conflict? Remember the exercise counting the number of "F"s? Conflict is going to exist. But we need to step back for a moment and examine our own perceptions of what is happening. We need to challenge our first impression of the coach's motivations for dealing with an athlete and see if we can understand the coach's position a little more. Only then will it be truly possible for us to have a successful conversation with the coach. Keep in mind the coach will probably feel threatened by parents. Parents also have a responsibility to listen and try to understand the other's point of view. By doing this, we may be able to discover solutions which allow everyone to maintain dignity while finding ways to make the athlete's experience much more positive.

WHAT YOUR KIDS ALWAYS WANTED TO TELL YOU, BUT WERE AFRAID TO SAY!

My last few years as an athletic director, I began asking our athletes about their experience of high school athletics. Specifically, I questioned them about the roles of their parents in their athletic experience. One day, I had a brainstorm to get feedback from them and share it with their parents. I asked three simple questions. First, "What do your parents do in your athletic experience that embarrasses you?" Secondly, "What are the things you really appreciate your parents doing in your athletic experience?" Finally, "If you knew I were talking with your parents tonight at a Parent Night, what would you like me to tell them about your athletic experience?"

The responses were fascinating and honest. Most parent groups are shocked and, at the same time, pleased to hear this information. It might be interesting for coaches to ask their own athletes these questions, compile the answers, and share them with parents. The coach must be careful, of course, to protect the anonymity of specific athletes. They need to know they are protected if they are to share freely.

Take a look at the following responses:

THINGS PARENTS DO THAT EMBARRASS THEIR KIDS!

- "Trying to teach me how to do something 'correctly' after a game."
- "Coaching during games even though you aren't the coach."
- "Telling me what I was doing wrong after every game."
- "Being asked to leave a field by an official."
- "Going crazy at the refs – because it is not your job. It is the coach's job to question bad calls."
- "Taunting other players, opponents, refs."
- "Yelling things at coaches and getting involved with something that was between the coach and me. It was none of their business."
- "Coming to a game drunk or after drinking."
- "Acting disappointed with what I am doing instead of reassuring me I will do better next time."
- "Getting a technical foul against our team."
- "Don't say, '(nickname), you really look cute in your uniform, honey'!"

Some of these scenarios are mind-boggling. We all know about parents who come to contests after drinking, but we sometimes forget how humiliating it can be for their son or daughter. The same could be said for parents who are asked to leave the field by an official because they were so out of control.

I have several times, including two times in one night, one at a girls' game, one in a boys' game, seen athletes running down the basketball court, looking into the stands, and either shouting or mouthing the words, "Shut up," to one of their out-of-control parents in the stands.

We all know how difficult it is for a coach to have parents "coaching" their athlete to do something differently than the coach is teaching it at practice. For a coach to ask a kid to pass the ball and for the parent to scream, "Shoot!" all the time, causes conflict in the athlete. For a parent to question the coach's ability or knowledge at the dinner table puts the athlete in the position of siding with the parent or with the coach. What a difficult position this is for a teenager! Do parents really want to do create this type of conflict?

THINGS PARENTS DO THAT THEIR KIDS REALLY APPRECIATE!

- "Taking time out of your busy schedules to come to games and support what we do."
- "Bringing snacks after a game."
- "Supporting the whole team, not just me."
- "Cheering the team even when losing badly."
- "Telling us we did a good job."
- "Being proud of us even when we didn't win."
- "Being quiet unless cheering with everyone else."
- "Never yelling at a coach or ref."
- "Making friends with the other parents."
- "Telling a "negative" parent to be quiet – Tootsie Roll Pop!"

We had one girl's basketball parent who will go down in "Awesome Parent History" for coming up with the "Tootsie Roll Pop" routine. She would bring a box of the candies into the gym. I never allowed food in the gym, but made an important exception for this mom. Whenever a parent got too loud or too out of control, whenever they shouted at the officials or at the opponents, this mom would reach into her cache and hand the parent a Tootsie Roll Pop. The first time or two, she had to make the obvious suggestion to the parent to put the Pop into his or her mouth. Within a very short time, parents understood clearly they were out of line if handed a Tootsie Roll Pop. Before long, parents would catch themselves and suggest out loud they might be better off calming down before they were handed one. No one ever took offense to being handed one and, before long, our parent crowd became very aware of the impact of their behavior and cheered more and more positively for our team, not against the other team.

Parents ought to get to know the parents of the other athletes on the team. Kids appreciate this. More importantly, it gives parents the very important knowledge needed to be a responsible parent. If we know the other parents in the stands, we can call them up and ask if there really is a party at their house this week or if someone is going to be home when the kids are visiting. It is difficult enough parenting today; we must take advantage of the help we can get by knowing the other parents.

ADVICE FROM THE KIDS TO YOU, THE PARENTS!

- ◆ "Don't get frustrated if I am not playing well or the team is losing."
- ◆ "Don't become too involved in our sports lives."
- ◆ "Stay in the stands and know your role."
- ◆ "Encourage regardless of performance."
- ◆ "We don't want parents trying to get us playing time. It should be between the player and the coach."
- ◆ "If I don't play, don't be angry with the coach or me."
- ◆ "Tell your kid not to steal."
- ◆ "Relax and let kids have fun."
- ◆ "Don't make a scene."
- ◆ "Remember it is our team"
- ◆ "It is not a life or death situation; it is just a game."

This is a very powerful set of suggestions. Every parent can learn from this advice. Kids want parents to treat them with respect. They want the parents to realize this is the athlete's experience, not the parents'. They want to be loved whether they played well or played poorly. They want to have FUN.

Kids love it when their parents come to watch them play. They also love it when they bring snacks and allow the athlete to enjoy the experience.

THE ABC'S OF PARENTING
IN THE 21ST CENTURY

Quit Awfulizing - "Ain't it terrible...!" "Can you believe what he did? What she said?" Worry never solved any problems. So resolve today to quit worrying and dwelling on the awful. Focus instead on enjoying the present and how today determines what tomorrow will bring. It is a very easy task to find someone who will agree how bad things are. Find those few who focus on how great things are despite all the hurdles out there.

Be positive. Raising a teen is a difficult job, one we were never really trained for. So why not focus on success rather than failure? After all, shouldn't we view success as an end result of failure?

Opportunity Cost – Anyone who has taken an economics class is reminded that when we choose one thing, the opportunity cost is what we did not choose. We have to give up something for something we thought was better. Your kids are who they are. There is not a whole lot of changing you can do. Remember all the wedding advice you got? Don't try to change your spouse. Accept him or her with all their faults. Focus on all their talents and the beautiful characteristics which attracted you in the first place. Focus on those positives which led you to the present situation, not on the possibilities had you made other choices; they are long gone.

Decide - then go for it. Make the best of it. Enjoy what is, not what could have been, as "what could have been" is often just a dream anyway.

Eat smart. See if you can't find a time to eat a meal together. The food and the company around the table make for healthy families.

Replace Fluids. We don't drink enough fluids to keep our bodies working right. Maybe replacing fluids also warns us about the type of fluids. Too much alcohol, caffeine, coffee? Maybe the message is an even broader one about helping our teens replace their choice of fluids with a healthier choice as well.

Get more sleep. Isn't this an obvious message for all of us?

Hugs - Be a parent, not a coach. Hug your kids even if it embarrasses them. They really like it and so do you.

Victory of "we" over "I." No family, no school, no team is successful when the focus is on the "I." Only when the "we" comes into play can there be success. "We" overcome things and achieve goals together, not alone. From the day you bring your sons and daughters home from the hospital, you focus on helping them become "we" people, focused on a world filled with others. Remember this is also true in the sports arena. When you talk around the dinner table about the "I" rather than the "we" of the team, you destroy team chemistry. The happiest moments of our lives are the "we" moments, the loneliest the "I" moments. Choose the "we."

Joy - Be cautious about taking life so seriously. We need to laugh more, to be playful more often. When we focus on tomorrow, the "what ifs," we find we often miss the humor and beauty of life around us today. Don't wait until tomorrow, or until you retire, or until the sun shines to have fun; start today, right now! Don't wait until it is too late.

Keep making forgiveness a habit. What is more important than forgiving? Over and over and over? Forgiveness means moving on, letting go of those things which are forgiven. We need to make a habit out of forgiveness. We claim it is OK to fail, that in failure we really learn the important lessons in life. If this is true, then we need to practice it by allowing failure to occur, then practicing forgiveness. Then growth can take place. Forgiveness means giving up control. As parents, we want to hold things over our kids' heads or those of their teachers or coaches, but this is not the message of forgiveness. Let it go.

Live this moment. We may have years and years with our kids or we may only have a few fleeting moments. We don't know. Choose to have no regrets later. Choose to smile rather than to frown. Choose life. Choose to enjoy every moment you can with your families. Choose it today.

Motivation. Understand why your teens do what they do. Their motivation may not always be the same as yours and it is OK. Parents of athletes often struggle with this concept: Maybe I was a good athlete and want my son or daughter to relive some of those moments for me; maybe I think an athletic scholarship might be an answer to the college question. Kids tend to resist the wisdom of our advice because they must experience life's journey themselves and often feel compelled to do the opposite of what we tell them. We must try to discover our son or daughter's motivation for doing what they do. Help them to develop and add maturity to their reasoning. The bottom line is we need to get out of the way and let them pursue their interests, certainly with our help, but also with the realization they must choose it for their own reasons. They may stumble along the way…that's OK.

Overcome Nausea. In cancer patients, nausea often accompanies life-saving treatments. The same is true for each of us in our daily grind. There are things that make us nauseous because this is not a perfect world. We can focus on the nausea and learn to dread the treatment or we can decide nausea is a sign my body is working to overcome the disease within me. You will get frustrated with your teens. You will get frustrated with the school or with a coach. Step back long enough to realize something healthy is taking place, even though at present you might feel queasy. Give the process a chance. Stand back a ways, remembering growth occurs best accompanied by failure.

Operate under new assumptions. Isn't it funny – we finally learn to be good parents about the time our children are grown and gone? What a waste. Too bad there isn't a class somewhere to teach us how to be the parent of a teen. What I do know, though, is success in parenting comes with updating our assumptions. Choose the "Road less traveled." What will you find? You will develop a team spirit because of entering the unknown together and knowing you need to work together to find your way. Anything that gets our teens to be our partner rather than our opponent is exciting.

Find a Positive support group. Avoid people who are constantly complaining. Find people who look for the positive in every situation. Consider yourself lucky if you find these people. Hang on to them. Be one yourself.

Ask Questions; get second opinions. Don't jump to conclusions. Don't make hasty decisions. Don't believe everything your child tells you. Just as there is bias present in our hearing what they are saying, there is a bias in their presentation of circumstances, too. Maybe the coach wasn't really as mean as you perceived, just maybe your athlete performed under expectation this particular day and needed a scapegoat. We all find it hard to admit we failed. How does the saying go? "If at first you don't succeed, find someone to blame!" Ask questions; check with the source; get a second opinion; allow for the filter of time.

Be Realistic—Reflect on the program and your Role in it -Not everyone can be the valedictorian or a Division I scholarship athlete. Not every team wins a state championship. Not every student gets a 1600 on the college SATs. A chain is as strong as its weakest link. We have all heard these dictums and you could probably recite many more. We need to accept who we are and what our skills are. We certainly need to work to improve them constantly, but we also have to accept there might be limits on what we can accomplish. Not every athlete is a star. A team cannot be successful without its role players. Help your kid to learn his or her role and do it better than anybody else. Help your athlete take pride in his or her accomplishments, however big or small they might be. Be realistic. Don't relive your career or put your expectations on their backs.

Focus on the "we" not the "I" so your experience, your role, will be much more positive.

Evaluate your Self-talk. What you say and what you do behind the scenes will have a huge effect on your teen. If you remind them how bad they are or how often they mess up, you will reinforce their behavior. Listen to the comments you make, the sarcasm you use to try to break through their teenage armor. Does it work? I would guess not if your experience is anything like mine. I suggest we ought to struggle with ourselves to focus on the positive. Tell our kids what they are doing right. Tell them when we are proud of their efforts. Be a good sport. Control your self-talk. Be positive.

Manage Toxic stress. Not all stress is bad. Much of what we accomplish is because of good stress which fills us with the adrenaline necessary and the motivation to finish a task. We all know the exhilaration of completing a task or a race, of accomplishing a climb or hike, of holding your child for the first time at birth, of walking down the aisle to become man and wife. Talk about stress! But it is the toxic stress, which causes us grief but really doesn't help us, that I am talking about. Worry is one of those. I know kids who worry so much about what they have to do that they never do anything. I know parents who spend so much time on the "what if…" game that they never sit back and enjoy the present moment. I know some who work so hard to make sure their kids never fail that they never learn to grow either. Find ways to manage those stresses you can't control. I remember Bobby Kennedy quoting Reinhold Niebuhr's Prayer of Serenity, "…*grant me the serenity to accept the things I cannot change, the courage to change the things I can, and the wisdom to know the difference.*"

Understand the partial remedy for "teengeritis"—Unity with other parents. I am convinced a teenager's goal is to keep parents from communicating. Has your teen ever told you you are the only parent who calls other parents or who sets curfews or the like? Has your teen ever reacted angrily when you mentioned you would call another parent to verify what they are doing? "What, you don't trust me?" My experience with teens is I can often do a better job of talking with yours than I can with my own. Yours will listen because I am not a threat. Get to know each other. Know who the parents of your kid's friends are. You'll learn a lot about your son or daughter by hearing how they act around other's homes. You'll gain an ally. You'll realize you are not the only parent in the world having trouble with teenagers. You might even gain some valuable insights and some proven techniques. Be unified; talk to each other. Besides, you will make some great friends in the process.

Values. I can tell you honestly I have doubted my ability to parent on numerous occasions. I have felt like a failure. It was only belief in those things in my life that I value which kept me going. I know I can't be a successful parent without others like you and I certainly can't do it without a strong personal belief that I am loved, even in my worst parenting moments. Values like faith, hope, and love must become real for us to succeed.

Why? Get beyond Why. Quit Whining. Alexis Herman, former United States Secretary of Labor, addressed a group of women in Seattle encouraging them to quit whining about the problems they are facing and start working on the solutions. We certainly want to know the answer to the question, "Why"? But we need to move beyond the "Why" to the solution. "Why" is a question that is often centered in the past. Why did this happen? Why did you do that? Why did you say that? It allows us to beat ourselves (or others) up for not acting differently in the past. I was once told we make decisions based on what we think was the best choice at a particular moment in time. We act in our best self-interest. Unfortunately, we do not always have all the necessary information at the time we choose. We may not know how someone else will react to what we do or say and regret it afterwards. But at the time, we thought we knew. Focusing on the past allows us to "feel good" as we beat people up for their choices. Why do kids do what they do? At the time, it sounded like a good idea, right? A better question I am told is, "What were you thinking at the time?" This is an attempt to understand the thinking process and to educate the thinker for the next choice. Get beyond the why.

EXude gratitude. Thank your spouse, thank your kids, thank your teachers, the coaches, thank the mail lady. How do you feel when someone says, "Thanks,

I really appreciate your efforts"? Does it hurt to say thanks? How do you feel when, one day out of the blue, your teenager says, "Thanks mom, thanks dad for the...."? Doesn't it pleasantly surprise you as our kids take us for granted most of the time? Give them a good model. Tell people how much their help means to you. Do it often.

"Yes" to helpful relationships. "No" to unhealthy ones. Do you have people in your life who take a lot of energy from you? They are nice and all, but they just take so much work? Faced with cancer and the possibility time might be limited, cancer patients are often told to focus on those relationships which bring them energy and to jettison those which drain their energy. Isn't the same true with us? We already have teens who take a lot of our energy, but bring us great joy at other times. What we don't need during this stage are others who drain us without renewing us. Don't we worry about our children's friends and watch for those who take, take, take? Look at your relationships and focus on those that have a healthy give and take, relationships which enhance your ability to parent, relationships that allow us to fail and to grow.

Live your life with Zest. We all learn the hard way that the only thing we know for sure is what we have TODAY. We had better enjoy it and make the best of every opportunity because there is no guarantee about TOMORROW. Your kids are critically important. They need you today. Tomorrow may be too late. Focus on them and their needs. Enjoy them. Read the books they are reading. If it is at all possible (and tolerable), listen to at least some of their music. Get to know their friends. Make your home a place where your kids and friends feel welcome to visit so you will know where your kids are, whom they are with, and what they are doing. Look and find the humor in our lot as parents of teens. Always remember, "This too will pass."

We have always thought it sad so many teenagers had to learn by their own experience rather than being able to learn from others. They could avoid so much pain by paying attention. But then they wouldn't be teenagers struggling to become their own persons in a difficult world, would they? "It will never happen to me" seems to be their attitude. Unfortunately, some of it will. So we as parents do our best to protect them from the big disasters. I hope you will never have to face one of those, but I also hope you will step back and allow them to experience an occasional "little" disaster. They will grow in the wisdom that is necessary to move into adulthood from these setbacks. Your love, values, and example will finally win out at about age 24. Be patient. Be vigilant. Have faith. Maintain hope. And most of all, Love. Do it today; do it now while you still have time.

LESSONS OF THE GENERATIONS

Everyone has stories to tell of how they learned life's lessons. Some lessons come without too much struggle, others with considerable pain and anguish. We need to develop an effective means of understanding who we are, why we do what we do, and how we best communicate with the important people in our lives. Parents of athletes have a particularly difficult task because they want the best for their sons and daughters. They want a great athletic experience mixed with a good dose of fun. In addition, they want their children to experience the successes associated with athletic competition.

Over the many years, it is easy to come to a simple, but powerful conclusion. Parents do what they do because they love their children! Everybody must know that, right? Coaches and Athletic Directors have difficulty with this one. Their experience of parents is often clouded by the parent's desire to get more playing time for their own athlete, even if it is at the expense of the team or other players. Often parents accuse the coach of all sorts of terrible things to try to get their way. All this is done, out of love, because the parents want their kids to be happy, to experience no pain. No one wants to sit around the dinner table at night with a teenager who is hurting because of a painful athletic experience, so parents sometimes step in to the fray. Parents need to recognize their own motivation when dealing with coaches so they know how to most appropriately respond.

Parents have a particularly difficult task. No one ever taught us how to be parents. There is no training period, only on-the-job training. There is no evaluation process as we go. Usually after our children are raised, we realize some of the things we wish we had done differently. To top it all off, our kids keep getting larger and smarter, thus forcing us to continually readjust our parental policies and procedures.

So how then do we speak with coaches about the delicate subject of our children and the conflicts which naturally arise in athletic participation? Consider the "Lessons of the Generations" in these hypothetical experiences. Can you find yourself or anyone you know in these examples? You will find many similarities to your own life and can substitute your own experience as well.

A FATHER

Imagine the father who exemplifies what it means to be a dedicated, loyal, responsible parent. He worked long hours his entire life to provide security for the family. He traveled in the early years as a salesman, often leaving early Monday morning and returning Friday evening. In the later years, he traveled by train into New York City from Connecticut, leaving early in the morning and arriving home in time for a late dinner.

The Son played three sports during his high school years and the father made attempts to get to as many contests as possible. Football provided the easiest opportunities to make games as they were played Saturday mornings. The dad volunteered for the Booster Club and ended up working most of the games either selling tickets or concessions.

After graduation the son went off to play college football and his dad attended every game he played over four years. After every game the son played, the dad came up to him, put his arm around his son and told him what a great game he had played – even after the games that did not go well.

Years later, when the son started coaching himself and raising children, he finally realized what his dad was really saying to him, "You already have a coach who will tell you what you did right and wrong in the game, what you need now is a parent who loves you no matter how you played!"

The dad understood what it meant to be a responsible and dutiful parent. He understood his place versus the coach's place. He instinctively knew that he should not interfere with the coach/athlete relationship by telling his son what he did right and wrong in the contest and what he should have done differently. Yet, he also liked to be in charge. The dad had been the captain of his college hockey team and certainly understood athletic competition, but he also knew and valued tradition, loyalty and fairness. He knew his role and he knew clearly what was not his role. As much as he liked to be in control of things, he also knew he needed to be supportive of the role of the coach by staying out of his domain. He demonstrated support to his son by making sure he knew his father was behind him, no matter what.

The Lesson – Parents like this understand Life is not always easy, that, as Vince Lombardi said, "It's not whether you get knocked down, it's whether you get up." Lombardi also has been so often misquoted concerning winning. He never said, "winning is the only thing." What he actually said was the same lesson the dad so often tried to teach, "Winning is not everything -- but making the effort to win is." The dad rewarded effort by letting his son know he was loved no matter how he played; that he had a parent available with whom he could celebrate or find sympathy and love. Be a parent (or guardian), not your child's "after practice coach".

THE SON

The son's kids began playing sports at a very young age. The son (we'll call him Tom) had been coaching for more than a decade when he often found himself coaching or assisting with his kids' sports teams. Both his son and daughter took up swimming competitively, possibly because they knew dad had no knowledge about the sport and they knew he couldn't coach it. The son's own son, we'll call him Kevin, would often ask his dad not to coach his teams because, if there ever came a time when a decision had to be made whether the coach's son or another player would go in the game, he knew his dad would always put the other kid in to avoid the appearance of bias.

By the time he grew to high school age, Kevin decided, like so many freshman boys, to try out for the football team. Since Tom had played both high school and college football, he thought this was great. Now what Tom seemed to miss was that Kevin was one of the three or four smallest kids on the team. He didn't play as often as Tom thought he ought to. When he did, Tom found himself analyzing every aspect of each play. Tom could tell Kevin what happened on every one of the few plays he played in each game. He could discuss with Kevin why the linebacker in front of him should have made the play that would have prevented him from having to make or miss a tackle. Tom found himself wearing blinders so Kevin was nearly the only player he saw on the field.

When games were over, Tom would drive Kevin home analyzing the game and trying to figure out what Kevin could have, should have, done differently. (Obviously he had not yet learned the lesson his own father tried to impart!) Tom felt his coaching and playing background gave him insight far and above what Kevin's freshman high school coaches had and imagined his son would be thrilled to have dad work with him. They began to have conflict over this, as you might imagine. Soon Tom's son didn't even want to talk about the game anymore. Tom remembered stories of some young athletes who stalled in the locker room after games as long as they could, so they didn't have to go home to replay the entire game that night with a parent. Then, he understood.

Until that point, Tom felt he clearly knew more about the game than either Kevin or his coaches did. After all, Tom had played and coached the sport for nearly 20 years, much longer than any of his son's young coaches. Tom knew he could help transform Kevin into a great football player if only he would listen. But this was the key – he didn't want to listen to his father.

Before too long, the fog began to lift from Tom's brain and he got the point. He went to his son and said, "I will no longer make a comment to you about your technique, the coach, or how you played the game, unless you ask a question. I know I have some skills and knowledge which might be helpful, but it is not my place to present it unless asked. From this day forward, I am going to just go and enjoy the opportunity to watch you play a game."

It wasn't often Kevin asked his father anything, but their relationship improved from that day forward. Kevin no longer had to deal with a dad who "knew it all" and made him feel dumb or who implied his coaches were dumb. He now had a dad who let him play and enjoy the game to the extent he wanted to, not the one dad wanted him to.

The Lesson – Tom needed to control his need to analyze and "fix" everything. He was way too intellectual and theoretical for his 14-year-old son. Tom enjoyed the strategy of the sport and enjoyed the challenge of finding solutions to problems. He expected perfection in himself and those around him, thus giving his son the impression he could never really measure up to dad's expectations. Tom needed to simply sit back and enjoy watching his son play and not feel the need to be in control, to be the standard setter for his son's activities or, for that matter, his life. Tom needed to let Kevin go, to allow him to play the sport for his reasons, to set his own goals, and to determine his own level of satisfaction with his participation. Tom needed to "release" Kevin. It was his choice to play, his experience to enjoy. Tom had already had his opportunity, now he needed to let his son go, to allow all consequences of his choices, positive and negative, and to thrill in his role as he watched Kevin grow.

THE SON'S DAUGHTER

The story of Tom's other child, daughter Colleen, is a great lesson for those we know who "live for the moment". These individuals can be master negotiators and natural entertainers who thrive on competition. Many of them are very successful athletes. One of the problems in athletics today is far too many athletes believe they will one day end up playing professionally, so why worry about academic success? Too often, they fail to see the advantage of working hard today so there are some payoffs years down the road when they might graduate from a college or university with a degree.

Colleen competed passionately and successfully at both the high school and collegiate levels. She was a five-time state champion in high school who received a scholarship to swim in college. She worked hard throughout her college years and competed in the Big East Championships and eventually was chosen as one of the captains for her college team. During her senior year, she continued to train and point toward the Big East Championships and a chance to qualify for the NCAA Championship Meet.

Then Tom's perspective on all this changed! In February of 1993, Tom sat at his desk in his office when the phone rang. Tom answered. With the first word out of the caller's mouth, his worst nightmare came true. As a parent, do you dread the possibility of that phone call in the middle of the night? Do you lie awake waiting for your children to arrive home after a date or activity? When Tom heard the voice, he instinctively knew something terrible had happened.

The voice was Colleen's college swim coach. Tom knew this was not a social call. The Coach took a deep breath and told Tom his daughter had just been diagnosed with lymphoma. Tom thanked the coach and Colleen got on the phone. She was in tears, as you might imagine, having just gotten the word herself. They talked; Tom assured Colleen everything would be all right, they would do whatever needed to be done to deal with this aggressively. Tom made her laugh and she believed everything would be OK, just as her dad had always told her. They agreed to speak again that night after the team doctor called with more information. Her swim career ended that very day.

To make a long story short, Tom learned more about cancer, and in particular Hodgkin's Disease, than he ever wanted to know. As a parent of a teenager, he knew what a difficult time of life he was dealing with each day. As a parent of a cancer patient, it hit home even more how precious each moment was. Tom knew there were days when his teenagers drove him nuts. Looking at his daughter and wondering how much time he had left with her really made him reevaluate his perception of his kids and his reactions to their "growth pains."

Today, Colleen is healthy, having survived with no recurrence for nearly a decade. She now has children of her own and values all she learned from this experience, though she would never want to try it again.

The Lesson – Two really important lessons came out of this experience. First, Tom learned there is something crucial about "appreciating the moment" that he, as a disciplined, hard worker who focused on the future, had never understood before this experience. The experience changed his life and caused him to try to appreciate the opportunities to enjoy people and experiences much more.

Secondly, this experience provided an outstanding example for those who "live for the moment" – there is a need to be prepared for the future. Colleen's encounter with cancer effectively ended her competitive career. She needed to be able to fall back on another option in her life. It demonstrated the critical nature of doing some planning for the future, for studying today for a reward which might only come several years down the road, for changing her way of thinking so she might experience life in some new and exciting ways. Athletics cannot be a "be all and end all." It is fun while it lasts, but it is not going to last forever. What will you do next?

THE SON'S GRANDDAUGHTER

Colleen's third daughter, Grace, was born with a chromosomal abnormality, IDIC 15. This means she has an extra chromosome, one that is a partial image of the 15th chromosome and that has a mirror image of the part incorrectly reproduced. To translate this into more understandable terms, she has this extra piece of a chromosome that will change the way she learns. Her parents have no idea whether this change will result in mild or severe learning disabilities and the doctors say only time and Grace herself will be able to tell how it will impact her life.

What Colleen does know is Grace, at age 18-months, is 6-8 months behind in development in most areas. She has to be taught every motion of every skill. She eventually picks up the skills, but mom has to manipulate her hands and knees, for instance, in a crawling motion to show her how it is done. She does not pick these skills up from watching the other girls or from experimenting. Everything must be taught.

Her parents do not know if Grace will ever be able to run or to kick a ball, whether she will be able to balance a checkbook or live on her own. They just don't know. But they are convinced, as Colleen says, Grace will be the most loved and hardest working kid with this problem. If there is a chance for her to live what is traditionally called a normal life, Grace will have every opportunity to do so.

The lesson – For parents like this, relationships are critical, in fact they are everything. The message is clear. Be thankful if your child has arms, legs, and a brain that functions as it was designed. Don't spend quite so much time worrying about whether your son or daughter will get into the right school, or play the right position, or get enough playing time. Enjoy the opportunity to watch the miracle they are as they run and jump and swim and play.

THE LESSONS' CONCLUSION

The Lessons of the Generations are clear.

Be your son or daughter's parent (or guardian), not their coach – they already have one of those, but desperately need a parent figure in their lives.

Let your children go – give them the opportunity to experience athletics without you directing it. You had your chance, now it is theirs. Khalil Gibran affirms this thought as he writes in a chapter in *The Prophet*:

CHILDREN

And a woman who held a babe against her bosom said,
"Speak to us of Children."
And he said:

> *Your children are not your children.*
> *They are the sons and daughters of Life's longing for itself.*
> *They come through you, but not from you.*
> *You may give them your love, but not your thoughts,*
> *For they have their own thoughts.*
> *You may house their bodies, but not their souls,*
> *For their souls dwell in the house of tomorrow,*
> *Which you cannot visit, not even in your dreams.*
> *You may strive to be like them, but seek not to make them like you.*
> *For life goes not backward nor tarries with yesterday.*
> *You are the bows from which your children as living arrows are*
>   *sent forth.*
> *The Archer sees the mark upon the path of the infinite, and He*
>   *bends you with his might that his arrows may go swift and far.*
> *Let your bending in the Archer's hand be for gladness:*
> *For even as He loves the arrow that flies, so He loves also the bow*
>   *that is stable.*

Help your children understand that, while "living for the moment" is an admirable trait, one which brings great joy, it is also critical to plan and prepare for tomorrow. Help your children understand the balance between appreciating the here and now and making sure they are ready for the day which follows.

Be thankful for every moment you have with your children. Appreciate the miracle they are. With so many possible genes and chromosomes in our bodies, we should be grateful everything works in their bodies the way nature designed them. Instead of worrying about whether your children are the leading scorer or the first or fifteenth off the bench, revel in the mystery of their ability and desire to even be a member of a team.

Parents need desperately to remember – each of us possesses the ability to learn from these lessons. Make the decision to step back, to remember that our perceptions of what our children are experiencing may not be exactly 100% accurate, and to enjoy the very short time span we have to watch our children experience the fun of athletic competition.

Sit back, relax, and enjoy athletics for what they are. Be a parent, let them go, teach them there is more to sports than winning, and be grateful for all the "little" things! Have fun!

CONCLUSION

What have we learned? Sports are our children's opportunity to learn about themselves, to challenge themselves, to grow in physical and emotional maturity, to learn new skills, to develop sportsmanship, and to more clearly understand a lot of life's lessons. Parents need to allow their children the opportunity to succeed on their own merit and to learn to fail with grace and dignity and to pick themselves up and try it all again.

We all need to be involved to a degree in our children's experience. We need to support them and to encourage them. But, most importantly, we have to let them go – let them experience it for themselves.

Kids play sports primarily to have fun. Let's all work together to make sure that the experience is an enjoyable one for all.

Let the kids play, the coaches coach, and the referees ref. Be a good sport always in all ways!

ABOUT THE AUTHOR

Tom Doyle served as a high school Athletic Director and taught History during his 30 year career in education. He coached football, baseball, basketball, and track. He is a past president and treasurer of the Washington state athletic director's association (WSSAAA). In 2001, he was recognized as Washington State's Athletic Director of the Year and is a 2005 inductee into the WSSAAA Hall of Fame. He presently serves as the District 2 Secretary of the Washington Interscholastic Activities Association (WIAA) and is a *True Colors* presenter.

Tom graduated from Colgate University in 1972 where he was a three-year varsity letterman in football and baseball. He earned a Masters degree (MAT) from Colgate in 1976. In 1993, he earned his Certified Athletic Administrator (CAA) credentials.

He taught at Seattle's O'Dea High School for three years before moving to Seattle Prep, a Jesuit High School, for the next 27 years. He held the positions of Department Head of Social Studies, Assistant Principal, and Activities Director. During his tenure as Seattle Prep's Athletic Director, over 75% of the student body participated in an extracurricular sport activity each year.

He currently is the business manager for Personal Perceptions Northwest (PPNW), providing *True Colors* presentations to businesses, schools, and teams throughout the Northwest. He speaks at Sport Parent Nights about the role of parents and sportsmanship, and has co-authored *True Coaching,* a book on effective coach, athlete, and parent communication. He is a certified instructor for City University where he teaches a course titled, "True Coaching: Effective Communication with Administrators, Coaches, Parents, and Athletes."

Tom and his wife of 30 years, Marilyn, learned many lessons as parents of two children, Colleen and Kevin, who competed in swimming, cross country, football and basketball. Their son-in-law, Jeff, is a successful high school swim coach. Tom has three granddaughters, Katie, Megan, and Grace.

ALSO AVAILABLE FROM SAN JUAN PUBLISHING

True Coaching: Effective Communication with Parents and Athletes
by Tom Doyle
    Practical strategies for coaches and athletic directors to meet the challenges
of athlete and parent communication.

ORDERING INFORMATION

The Sport Parent's Manual by Tom Doyle $8.95

True Coaching: Effective Communication with Parents and Athletes
by Tom Doyle $16.95

Washington State residents include 8.8% sales tax.
Add $3.00 for shipping & handling.
Special school and quantity pricing available upon request.

SAN JUAN PUBLISHING
PO Box 923
Woodinville, WA 98072
(425) 485-2813
sanjuanbooks@yahoo.com
www.sanjuanbooks.com